Favourite Hym

Music arranged and processed by Barnes Music Engraving Ltd
East Sussex TN22 4HA, UK

Cover design by xheight design limited

Published 1996

International
MUSIC
Publications

International Music Publications Limited
Griffin House 161 Hammersmith Road London W6 8BS England

Abide With Me

Words by H F Lyte / Music by W H Monk

Suggested Registration: Flute
Rhythm: Soft Rock
Tempo: ♩ = 88

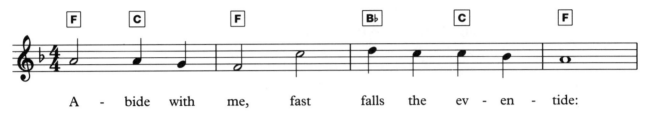

A - bide with me, fast falls the ev - en - tide:

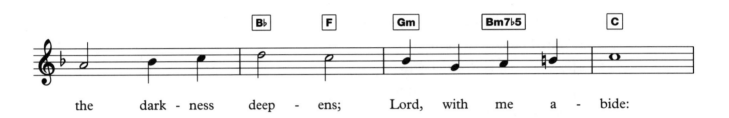

the dark - ness deep - ens; Lord, with me a - bide:

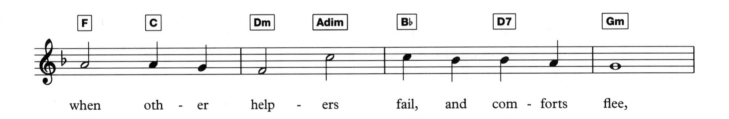

when oth - er help - ers fail, and com - forts flee,

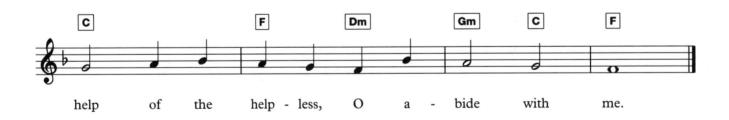

help of the help - less, O a - bide with me.

1   Abide with me, fast falls the eventide:
     the darkness deepens; Lord, with me abide:
     when other helpers fail, and comforts flee,
     help of the helpless, O abide with me.

2   Swift to its close ebbs out life's little day;
     earth's joys grow dim, its glories pass away;
     change and decay in all around I see:
     O thou who changest not, abide with me.

3   I need thy presence every passing hour;
     what but thy grace can foil the tempter's power?
     who like thyself my guide and stay can be?
     through cloud and sunshine, Lord, abide with me.

4   Hold thou thy cross before my closing eyes:
     shine through the gloom, and point me to the skies:
     heaven's morning breaks, and earth's vain shadows flee;
     in life, in death, O Lord, abide with me.

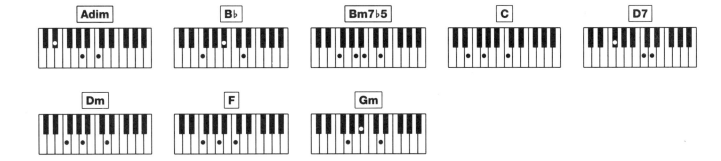

All Glory, Laud, And Honour

Original Words by St Theodulph of Orleans / English Words by J M Neale / Music adapted from M Teschner

Suggested Registration: French Horn
Rhythm: Soft Rock
Tempo: ♩ = 100

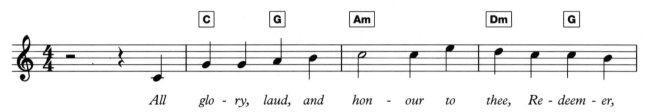

All glo - ry, laud, and hon - our to thee, Re - deem - er,

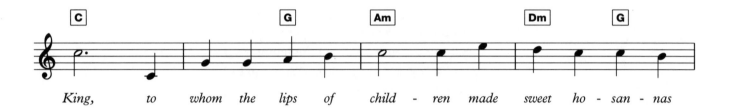

King, to whom the lips of child - ren made sweet ho - san - nas

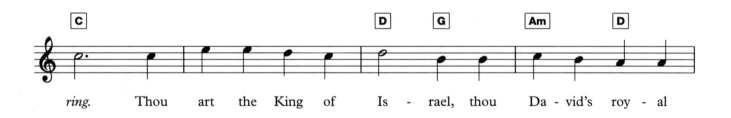

ring. Thou art the King of Is - rael, thou Da - vid's roy - al

Son, who in the Lord's name com - est, the King and bles - sèd one:

All glory, laud, and honour
to thee, Redeemer, King,
to whom the lips of children
made sweet hosannas ring.

1   Thou art the King of Israel,
     thou David's royal Son,
     who in the Lord's name comest,
     the King and blessèd one:

2   The company of angels
     are praising thee on high,
     and mortal men and all things
     created make reply:

3   The people of the Hebrews
     with palms before thee went:
     our praise and prayer and anthems
     before thee we present:

4   To thee before thy passion
     they sang their hymns of praise:
     to thee now high exalted
     our melody we raise:

5   Thou didst accept their praises,
     accept the prayers we bring,
     who in all good delightest,
     thou good and gracious King:

6   For homage may we bring thee
     our victory o'er the foe,
     that in the Conqueror's triumph
     this strain may ever flow:

     All glory . . .

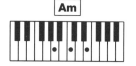
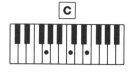
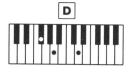
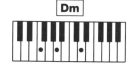
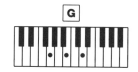

All People That On Earth Do Dwell

Words by W Kethe / Music from *Genevan Psalter*

Suggested Registration: Pipe Organ
Rhythm: Soft Rock
Tempo: ♩ = 100

All peo - ple that on earth do

dwell, sing to the Lord with cheer - ful

voice; him serve with fear, his praise forth

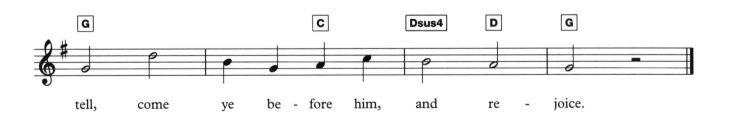

tell, come ye be - fore him, and re - joice.

1   All people that on earth do dwell,
    sing to the Lord with cheerful voice;
    him serve with fear, his praise forth tell,
    come ye before him, and rejoice.

2   The Lord, ye know, is God indeed;
    without our aid he did us make;
    we are his folk, he doth us feed,
    and for his sheep he doth us take.

3   O enter then his gates with praise,
    approach with joys his courts unto;
    praise, laud and bless his name always,
    for it is seemly so to do.

4   For why? The Lord our God is good:
    his mercy is for ever sure;
    his truth at all times firmly stood,
    and shall from age to age endure.

5   To Father, Son, and Holy Ghost,
    the God whom heaven and earth adore,
    from men and from the angel-host
    be praise and glory evermore.

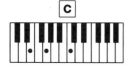 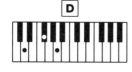 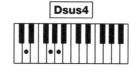 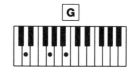

All Things Bright And Beautiful

Words by Cecil Frances Alexander / Music by W H Monk

Suggested Registration: Flute
Rhythm: Soft Rock
Tempo: ♩ = 112

All things bright and beau - ti - ful, all crea - tures great and small,

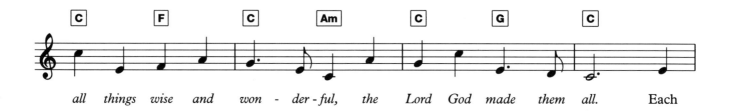

all things wise and won - der - ful, the Lord God made them all. Each

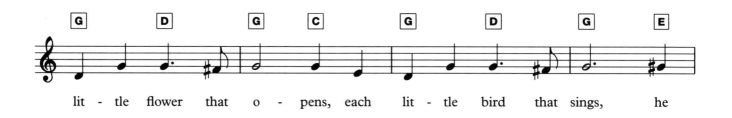

lit - tle flower that o - pens, each lit - tle bird that sings, he

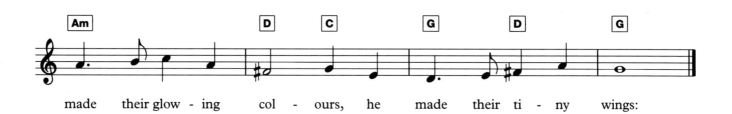

made their glow - ing col - ours, he made their ti - ny wings:

All things bright and beautiful,
all creatures great and small,
all things wise and wonderful,
the Lord God made them all.

1   Each little flower that opens,
    each little bird that sings,
    he made their glowing colours,
    he made their tiny wings:

2   The purple-headed mountain,
    the river running by,
    the sunset, and the morning
    that brightens up the sky:

3   The cold wind in the winter
    the pleasant summer sun,
    the ripe fruits in the garden,
    he made them every one:

4   The tall trees in the greenwood,
    the meadows where we play,
    the rushes by the water:
    we gather every day:

5   He gave us eyes to see them,
    and lips that we might tell
    how great is God almighty
    who has made all things well:

    All things bright . . .

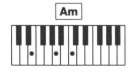
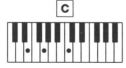
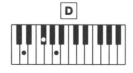
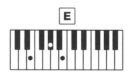
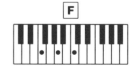

Alleluya, Sing To Jesus

Words by W Chatterton Dix / Music by R H Pritchard

Suggested Registration: Strings
Rhythm: Waltz
Tempo: ♩ = 100

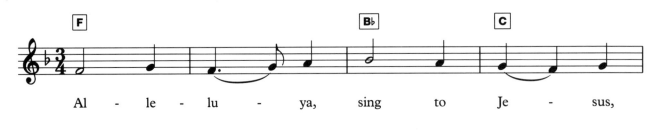

Al - le - lu - ya, sing to Je - sus,

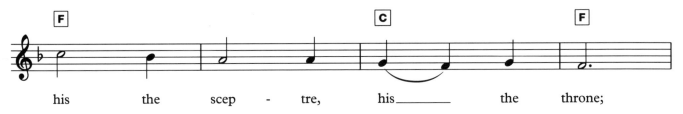

his the scep - tre, his_____ the throne;

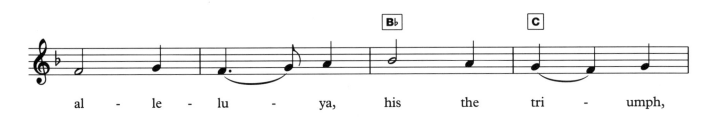

al - le - lu - ya, his the tri - umph,

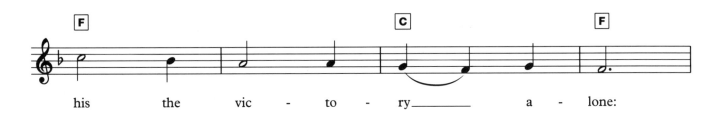

his the vic - to - ry_____ a - lone:

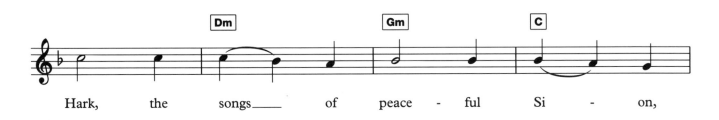

Hark, the songs_____ of peace - ful Si - on,

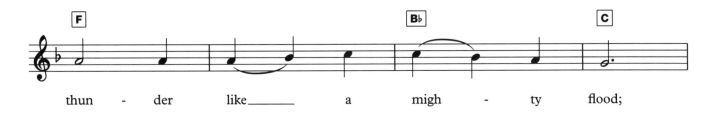

thun - der like_____ a migh - ty flood;

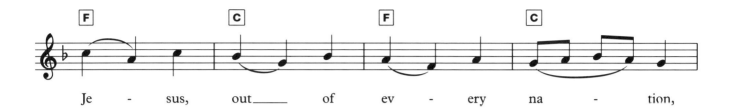

Je - sus, out____ of ev - ery na - tion,

hath re - deemed____ us by his blood.

1 Alleluya, sing to Jesus,
his the sceptre, his the throne;
alleluya, his the triumph,
his the victory alone:
Hark, the songs of peaceful Sion,
thunder like a mighty flood;
Jesus, out of every nation,
hath redeemed us by his blood.

2 Alleluya, not as orphans
are we left in sorrow now;
alleluya, he is near us,
faith believes, nor questions how;
though the cloud from sight received him
when the forty days were o'er,
shall our hearts forget his promise,
'I am with you evermore?'

3 Alleluya, bread of angels,
thou on earth, our food, our stay;
alleluya, here the sinful
flee to thee from day to day;
intercessor, friend of sinners,
earth's Redeemer, plead for me,
where the songs of all the sinless
sweep across the crystal sea.

4 Alleluya, King eternal,
thee the Lord of lords we own;
alleluya, born of Mary,
earth thy footstool, heaven thy throne:
Thou within the veil hast entered,
robed in flesh, our great high priest;
thou on earth both priest and victim
in the eucharistic feast.

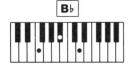
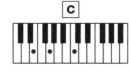
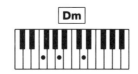
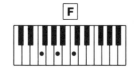
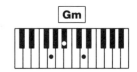

As With Gladness Men Of Old

Words by W Chatterton Dix / Music adapted from C Kocher by W H Monk

Suggested Registration: Acoustic Guitar
Rhythm: Soft Rock
Tempo: ♩ = 100

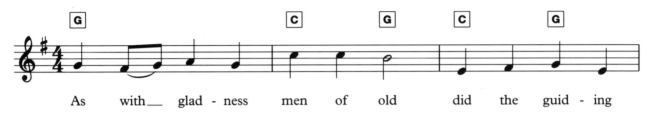

As with__ glad - ness men of old did the guid - ing

star be - hold, as with__ joy they hailed its light,

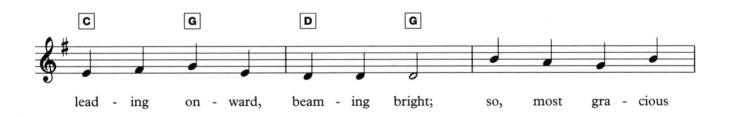

lead - ing on - ward, beam - ing bright; so, most gra - cious

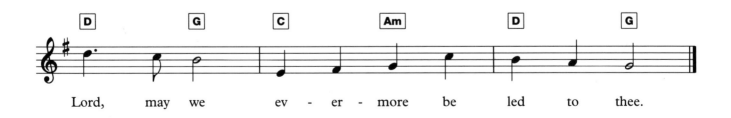

Lord, may we ev - er - more be led to thee.

1   As with gladness men of old
did the guiding star behold,
as with joy they hailed its light,
leading onward, beaming bright;
so, most gracious Lord, may we
evermore be led to thee.

2   As with joyful steps they sped,
Saviour, to thy lowly bed,
there to bend the knee before
thee whom heaven and earth adore;
so may we with willing feet
ever seek thy mercy-seat.

3   As they offered gifts most rare
at thy cradle rude and bare,
so may we with holy joy,
pure and free from sin's alloy,
all our costliest treasure's bring,
Christ, to thee our heavenly King.

4   Holy Jesus, every day
keep us in the narrow way,
and, when earthly things are past,
bring our ransomed souls at last
where they need no star to guide,
where no clouds thy glory hide.

5   In the heavenly country bright
need they no created light;
thou its light, its joy, its crown,
thou its sun which goes not down;
there for ever may we sing
alleluias to our King.

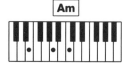
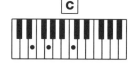
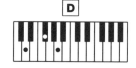
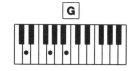

Be Thou My Vision

Irish traditional

Suggested Registration: Strings
Rhythm: Waltz
Tempo: ♩ = 92

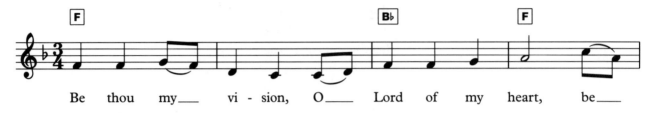

Be thou my___ vi - sion, O___ Lord of my heart, be___

all else but naught to me, save that thou art; be

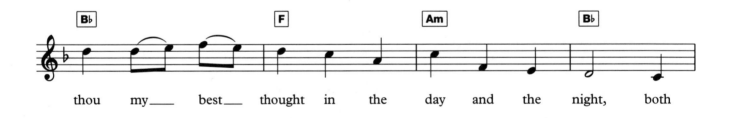

thou my___ best___ thought in the day and the night, both

wak - ing and sleep - ing, thy___ pre - sence my light.

1   Be thou my vision, O Lord of my heart,
     be all else but naught to me, save that thou art;
     be thou my best thought in the day and the night,
     both waking and sleeping, thy presence my light.

2   Be thou my wisdom, be thou my true word,
     be thou ever with me, and I with thee, Lord;
     be thou my great Father, and I thy true son;
     be thou in me dwelling, and I with thee one.

3   Be thou my breastplate, my sword for the fight;
     be thou my whole armour, be thou my true might;
     be thou my soul's shelter, be thou my strong tower:
     O raise thou me heavenward, great Power of my power.

4   Riches I heed not, nor man's empty praise:
     be thou mine inheritance now and always;
     be thou and thou only the first in my heart;
     O Sovereign of heaven, my treasure thou art.

5   High King of heaven, thou heaven's bright Sun,
     O grant me its joys after vict'ry is won;
     great Heart of my own heart, whatever befall,
     still be thou my vision, O ruler of all.

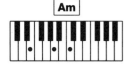 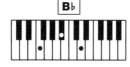 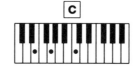 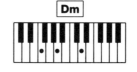 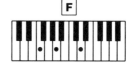

Breathe On Me, Breath Of God

Words by Edwin Hatch / Music by C Lockhart

Suggested Registration: Flute
Rhythm: Soft Rock
Tempo: ♩ = 92

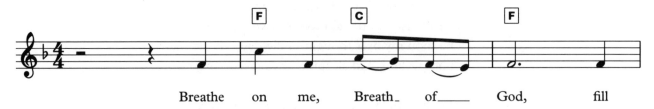

Breathe on me, Breath of God, fill

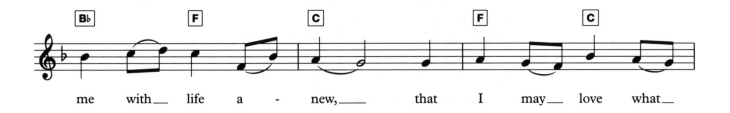

me with life a - new, that I may love what

thou dost love, and do what thou wouldst do.

1   Breathe on me, Breath of God,
    fill me with life anew,
    that I may love what thou dost love,
    and do what thou wouldst do.

2   Breathe on me, Breath of God,
    until my heart is pure;
    until with thee I will one will,
    to do and to endure.

3   Breathe on me, Breath of God,
    till I am wholly thine;
    until this earthly part of me
    glows with thy fire divine.

4   Breathe on me, Breath of God,
    so shall I never die,
    but live with thee the perfect life
    of thine eternity.

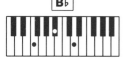
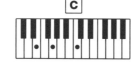
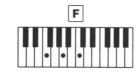

Brightest And Best

Words by Bishop R Heber / Music by F J Thrupp

Suggested Registration: Pipe Organ
Rhythm: Soft Rock
Tempo: ♩ = 132

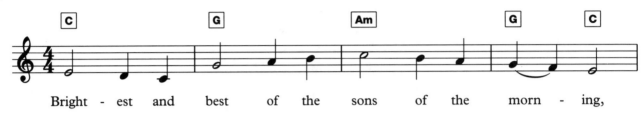

Bright - est and best of the sons of the morn - ing,

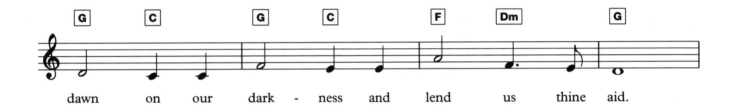

dawn on our dark - ness and lend us thine aid.

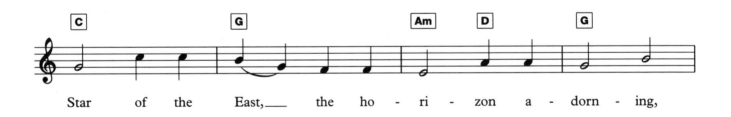

Star of the East,___ the ho - ri - zon a - dorn - ing,

guide where our in - fant Re - deem - er is laid.

1   Brightest and best of the sons of the morning,
    dawn on our darkness and lend us thine aid.
    Star of the East, the horizon adorning,
    guide where our infant Redeemer is laid.

2   Cold on his cradle the dew-drops are shining,
    low lies his head with the beasts of the stall:
    angels adore him in slumber reclining,
    Maker and Monarch and Saviour of all.

3   Say, shall we yield him, in costly devotion,
    odours of Edom and offerings divine?
    Gems of the mountain and pearls of the ocean,
    myrrh from the forest or gold from the mine?

4   Vainly we offer each ample oblation,
    vainly with gifts would his favour secure;
    richer by far is the heart's adoration,
    dearer to God are the prayers of the poor.

5   Brightest and best of the sons of the morning,
    dawn on our darkness and lend us thine aid.
    Star of the East, the horizon adorning,
    guide where our infant Redeemer is laid.

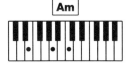
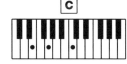
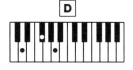
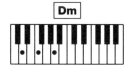
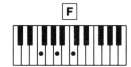
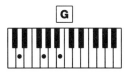

The Day Thou Gavest

Words by J Ellerton / Music by C C Scholefield

Suggested Registration: Pipe Organ
Rhythm: Waltz
Tempo: ♩ = 100

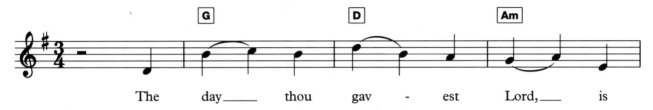

The day____ thou gav - est Lord,____ is

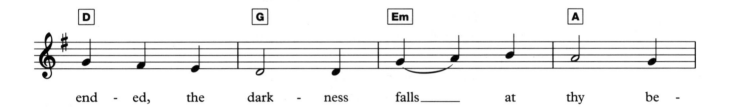

end - ed, the dark - ness falls____ at thy be -

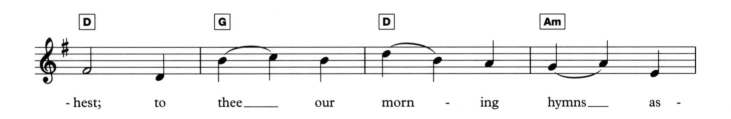

- hest; to thee____ our morn - ing hymns____ as -

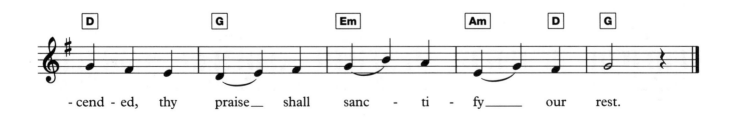

- cend - ed, thy praise__ shall sanc - ti - fy____ our rest.

1 The day thou gavest Lord, is ended,
  the darkness falls at thy behest;
  to thee our morning hymns ascended,
  thy praise shall sanctify our rest.

2 We thank thee that thy Church unsleeping,
  while earth rolls onward into light,
  through all the world her watch is keeping,
  and rests not now by day or night.

3 As o'er each continent and island
  the dawn leads on another day,
  the voice of prayer is never silent,
  nor dies the strain of praise away.

4 The sun that bids us rest is waking
  our brethren 'neath the western sky,
  and hour by hour fresh lips are making
  thy wondrous doings heard on high.

5 So be it, Lord, thy throne shall never,
  like earth's proud empires, pass away;
  thy kingdom stands, and grows for ever,
  till all thy creatures own thy sway.

A
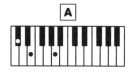

Am

C
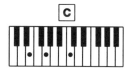

D
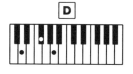

Em
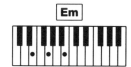

G
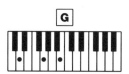

Dear Lord And Father Of Mankind

Words by J G Whittier / Music by C Hubert H Parry

Suggested Registration: Strings
Rhythm: Soft Rock
Tempo: ♩ = 88

Dear Lord and Fa - ther___ of man-kind, for -

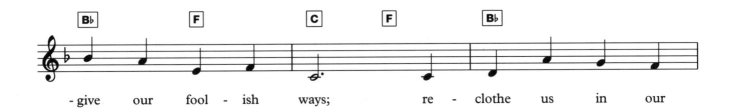

- give our fool - ish ways; re - clothe us in our

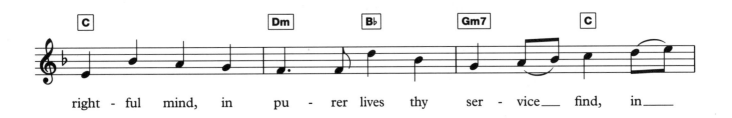

right - ful mind, in pu - rer lives thy ser - vice___ find, in___

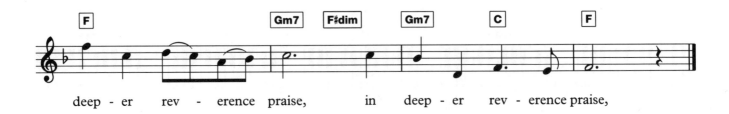

deep - er rev - erence praise, in deep - er rev - erence praise,

1   Dear Lord and Father of mankind,
     forgive our foolish ways;
     reclothe us in our rightful mind,
     in purer lives thy service find,
     in deeper reverence praise.

2   In simple trust like theirs who heard,
     beside the Syrian sea,
     the gracious calling of the Lord,
     let us, like them, without a word
     rise up and follow thee.

3   O Sabbath rest by Galilee!
     O calm of hills above,
     where Jesus knelt to share with thee
     the silence of eternity,
     interpreted by love!

4   Drop thy still dews of quietness,
     till all our strivings cease;
     take from our souls the strain and stress,
     and let our ordered lives confess
     the beauty of thy peace.

5   Breathe through the heats of our desire
     thy coolness and thy balm;
     let sense be dumb, let flesh retire;
     speak through the earthquake, wind, and fire,
     O still small voice of calm.

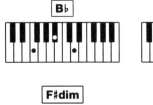  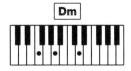 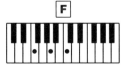 

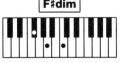 

FIGHT THE GOOD FIGHT

Words by J S B Monsell / Music by J Hatton

Suggested Registration: French Horn
Rhythm: Soft Rock
Tempo: ♩ = 126

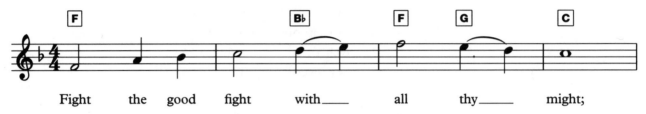

Fight the good fight with___ all thy___ might;

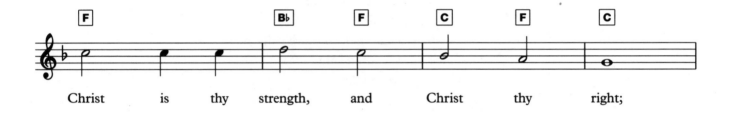

Christ is thy strength, and Christ thy right;

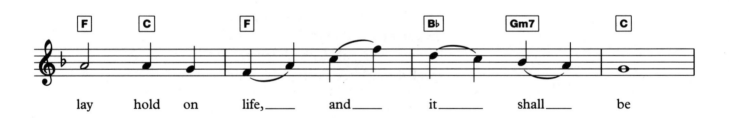

lay hold on life,___ and___ it___ shall___ be

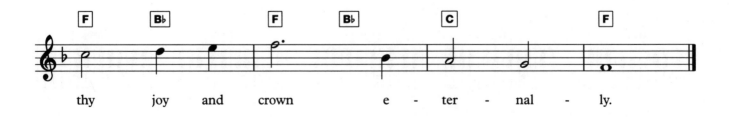

thy joy and crown e - ter - nal - ly.

1   Fight the good fight with all thy might;
     Christ is thy strength, and Christ thy right;
     lay hold on life, and it shall be
     thy joy and crown eternally.

2   Run the straight race through God's good grace,
     lift up thine eyes, and seek his face;
     life with its way before us lies;
     Christ is the path, and Christ the prize.

3   Cast care aside, lean on thy guide;
     his boundless mercy will provide;
     trust, and thy trusting soul shall prove
     Christ is its life, and Christ its love.

4   Faint not nor fear, his arms are near;
     he changeth not, and thou art dear,
     only believe, and thou shalt see
     that Christ is all in all to thee.

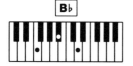
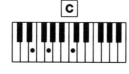
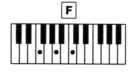
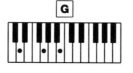

Jesus Christ Is Risen Today

From *Lyra Davidica, 1708*

Suggested Registration: Pipe Organ
Rhythm: Soft Rock
Tempo: ♩ = 108

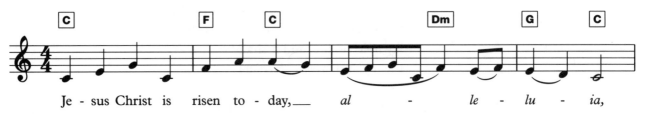

Je - sus Christ is risen to - day,___ al - le - lu - ia,

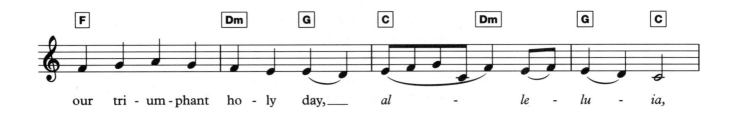

our tri - um - phant ho - ly day,___ al - le - lu - ia,

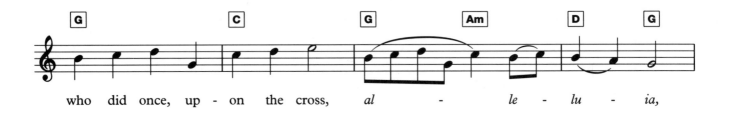

who did once, up - on the cross, al - le - lu - ia,

suf - fer___ to re - deem our loss,___ al - le - lu - ia.

1   Jesus Christ is risen today, *alleluia,*
     our triumphant holy day, *alleluia,*
     who did once, upon the cross, *alleluia,*
     suffer to redeem our loss, *alleluia.*

2   Hymns of praise then let us sing *alleluia,*
     unto Christ, our heavenly King, *alleluia,*
     who endured the Cross and grave, *alleluia,*
     sinners to redeem and save, *alleluia.*

3   But the pains that he endured, *alleluia,*
     our salvation have procured; *alleluia,*
     now above the sky he's King, *alleluia,*
     where the angels ever sing, *alleluia.*

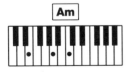
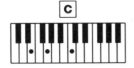
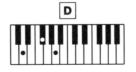
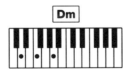
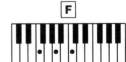
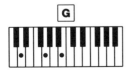

Jesus, Good Above All Other

Traditional

Suggested Registration: Flute
Rhythm: Waltz
Tempo: ♩ = 108

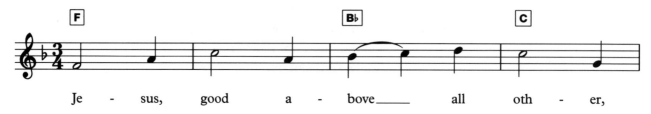

Je - sus, good a - bove___ all oth - er,

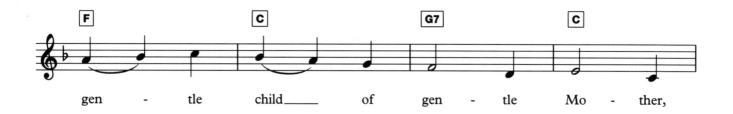

gen - tle child___ of gen - tle Mo - ther,

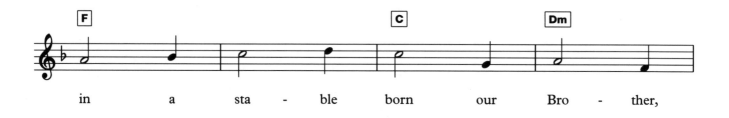

in a sta - ble born our Bro - ther,

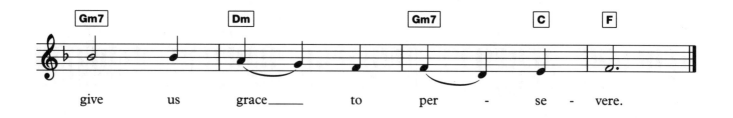

give us grace___ to per - se - vere.

1   Jesus, good above all other,
     gentle child of gentle Mother,
     in a stable born our Brother,
     give us grace to persevere.

2   Jesus, cradled in a manger,
     for us facing every danger,
     living as a homeless stranger,
     make we thee our King most dear.

3   Jesus, for thy people dying,
     risen Master, death defying,
     Lord in heaven, thy grace supplying,
     keep us to thy presence near.

4   Jesus, who our sorrows bearest,
     all our thoughts and hopes thou sharest,
     thou to man the truth declarest,
     help us all thy truth to hear.

5   Lord, in all our doings guide us;
     pride and hate shall ne'er divide us;
     we'll go on with thee beside us,
     and with joy we'll persevere!

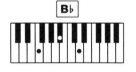 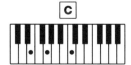 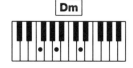 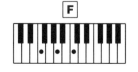 

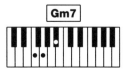

Lead Us, Heavenly Father, Lead Us

Words by J Edmeston / Music adapted from F Filitz's *Choralbuch*

Suggested Registration: Pipe Organ
Rhythm: Soft Rock
Tempo: ♩ = 100

Lead us, heaven - ly Fa - ther, lead us o'er the world's tem -

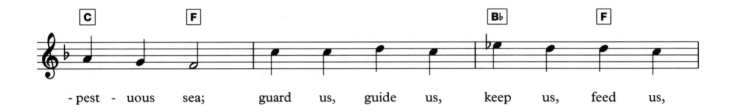

- pest - uous sea; guard us, guide us, keep us, feed us,

for we have no help but thee; yet pos - sess - ing

ev - ery bless - ing, if our God our Fa - ther be.

1   Lead us, heavenly Father, lead us
     o'er the world's tempestuous sea;
     guard us, guide us, keep us, feed us,
     for we have no help but thee;
     yet possessing every blessing,
     if our God our Father be.

2   Saviour, breathe forgiveness o'er us:
     all our weakness thou dost know;
     thou didst tread this earth before us,
     thou didst feel its keenest woe;
     lone and dreary, faint and weary,
     through the desert thou didst go.

3   Spirit of our God, descending,
     fill our hearts with heavenly joy,
     love with every passion blending,
     pleasure that can never cloy:
     thus provided, pardoned, guided,
     nothing can our peace destroy.

 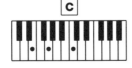 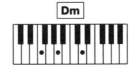 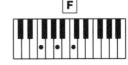 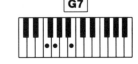

Love Divine, All Loves Excelling

Words by Charles Wesley / Music by John Stainer

Suggested Registration: Pipe Organ
Rhythm: Soft Rock
Tempo: ♩ = 84

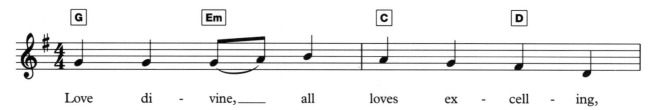

Love di - vine,___ all loves ex - cell - ing,

joy of heaven, to earth come down, fix in us___ thy

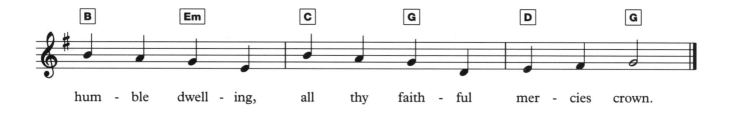

hum - ble dwell - ing, all thy faith - ful mer - cies crown.

1   Love divine, all loves excelling,
    joy of heaven, to earth come down,
    fix in us thy humble dwelling,
    all thy faithful mercies crown.

2   Jesu, thou art all compassion,
    pure unbounded love thou art;
    visit us with thy salvation,
    enter every trembling heart.

3   Come, almighty to deliver,
    let us all thy grace receive;
    suddenly return, and never,
    never more thy temples leave.

4   Thee we would be always blessing,
    serve thee as thy hosts above;
    pray, and praise thee, without ceasing,
    glory in thy perfect love.

5   Finish then thy new creation:
    pure and spotless let us be;
    let us see thy great salvation,
    perfectly restored in thee;

6   Changed from glory into glory,
    till in heaven we take our place,
    till we cast our crowns before thee,
    lost in wonder, love and praise.

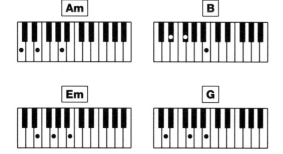

Majesty

Words and Music by Jack Hayford

Suggested Registration: Piano
Rhythm: Soft Rock
Tempo: ♩ = 120

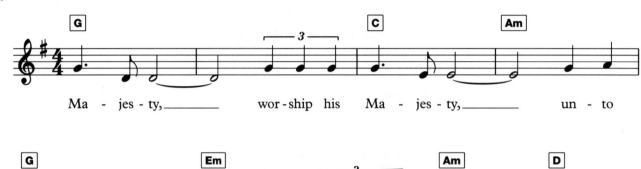

Ma - jes - ty,_____ wor - ship his Ma - jes - ty,_____ un - to

Je - sus be glo - ry, hon - our and praise._____

Ma - jes - ty,_____ king-dom, au - tho - ri - ty_____ flows from his

throne un - to his own, his an - them raise._____ So ex -

- alt, lift up on high the name of Je - sus,_____ mag - ni -

- fy, come glo - ri - fy, Christ Je - sus the King._____

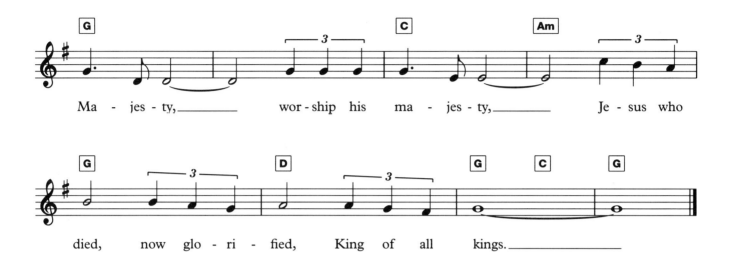

Ma - jes - ty,_____ wor - ship his ma - jes - ty,_____ Je - sus who

died, now glo - ri - fied, King of all kings._____

Majesty, worship his Majesty,
unto Jesus be glory, honour and praise.
Majesty, kingdom, authority
flows from his throne unto his own,
his anthem raise.

So exalt, lift up on high the name of Jesus,
magnify, come glorify, Christ Jesus the King.
Majesty, worship his majesty,
Jesus who died, now glorified,
King of all kings.

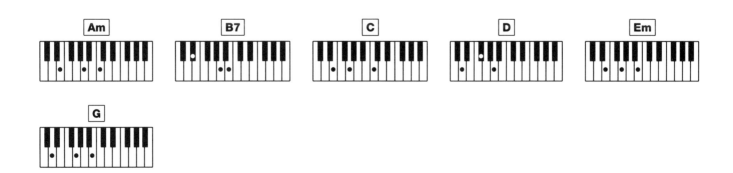

O Jesus, I Have Promised

Words by J E Bode / Music by S S Wesley

Suggested Registration: Strings
Rhythm: Soft Rock
Tempo: ♩ = 96

O Je-sus, I have prom-ised to serve thee to the

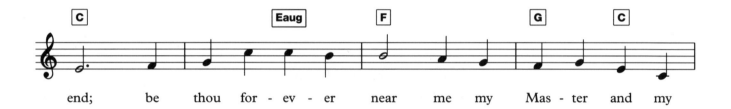

end; be thou for-ev-er near me my Mas-ter and my

Friend; I shall not fear the bat-tle if thou art by my

side, nor wan-der from the path-way if thou wilt be my Guide.

1   O Jesus, I have promised
    to serve thee to the end;
    be thou forever near me
    my Master and my Friend;
    I shall not fear the battle
    if thou art by my side,
    nor wander from the pathway
    if thou wilt be my Guide.

2   O let me feel thee near me:
    the world is ever near;
    I see the sights that dazzle,
    the tempting sounds I hear;
    my foes are ever near me,
    around me and within;
    but Jesus, draw thou nearer,
    and shield my soul from sin.

3   O let me hear thee speaking
    in accents clear and still,
    above the storms of passion,
    the murmurs of self-will;
    O speak to reassure me,
    to hasten or control;
    O speak, and make me listen,
    thou Guardian of my soul.

4   O Jesus, thou hast promised
    to all who follow thee,
    that where thou art in glory
    there shall thy servant be;
    And, Jesus, I have promised
    to serve thee to the end;
    O give me grace to follow,
    My Master and my Friend.

5   O let me see thy footmarks,
    and in them plant mine own;
    my hope to follow duly
    is in thy strength alone:
    O guide me, call me, draw me,
    uphold me to the end;
    and then in heaven receive me,
    My Saviour and my Friend.

Am
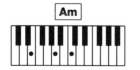

C
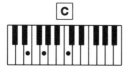

Dm
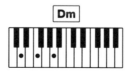

Eaug
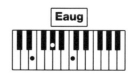

F
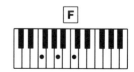

G
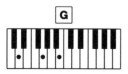

ONWARD, CHRISTIAN SOLDIERS

Words by S Baring-Gould / Music by Arthur Sullivan

Suggested Registration: French Horn
Rhythm: March
Tempo: ♩ = 116

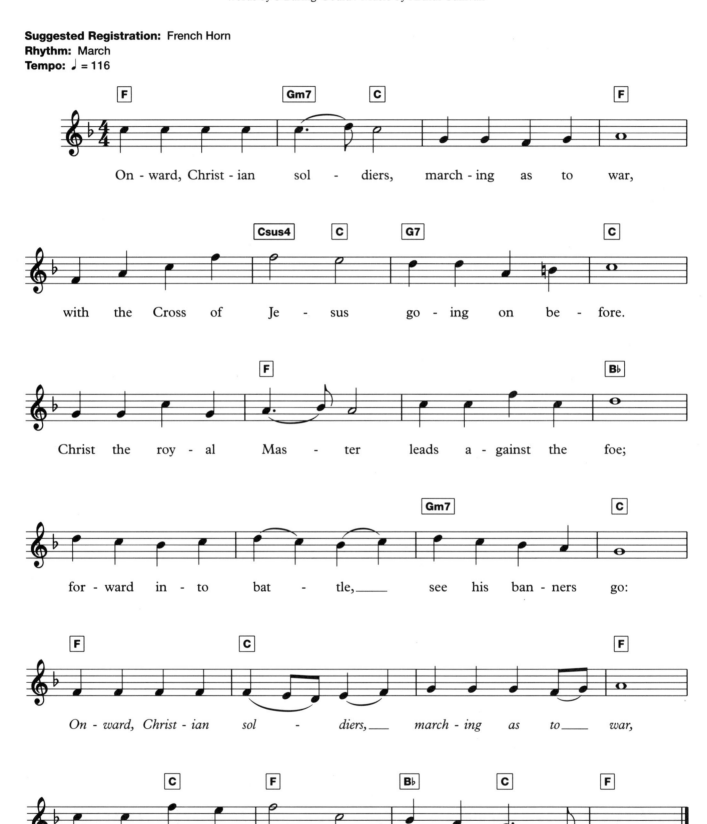

© 1996 International Music Publications Limited, Woodford Green, Essex IG8 8HN

1 Onward, Christian soldiers,
marching as to war,
with the Cross of Jesus
going on before.
Christ the royal Master
leads against the foe;
forward into battle,
see his banners go:

Onward, Christian soldiers,
marching as to war,
with the Cross of Jesus
going on before.

2 At the sign of triumph
Satan's host doth flee;
on then, Christian soldiers,
on to victory.
Hell's foundations quiver
at the shout of praise;
brothers, lift your voices,
loud your anthems raise:

Onward . . .

3 Like a mighty army
moves the Church of God;
brothers, we are treading
where the saints have trod:
we are not divided,
all one body we,
one in hope and doctrine,
one in charity:

Onward . . .

4 Crowns and thrones may perish,
kingdoms rise and wane,
but the Church of Jesus
constant will remain:
gates of hell can never
'gainst that Church prevail;
we have Christ's own promise,
and that cannot fail:

Onward . . .

5 Onward then, ye people,
join our happy throng,
blend with ours your voices
in the triumph song:
glory, laud, and honour
unto Christ the King,
this through countless ages
men and angels sing:

Onward . . .

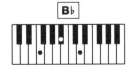
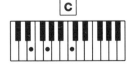
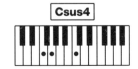
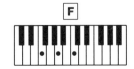

THERE IS A GREEN HILL FAR AWAY

Words by Cecil Frances Alexander / Music by W Horsley

Suggested Registration: Pipe Organ
Rhythm: Soft Rock
Tempo: ♩ = 84

There is a green hill far a - way, with -

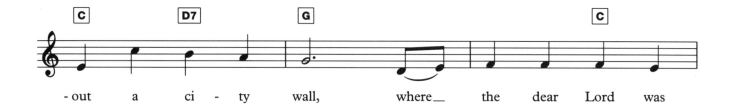

- out a ci - ty wall, where___ the dear Lord was

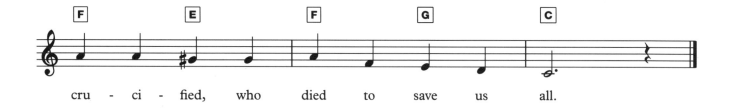

cru - ci - fied, who died to save us all.

1   There is a green hill far away,
    without a city wall,
    where the dear Lord was crucified,
    who died to save us all.

2   We may not know, we cannot tell,
    what pains he had to bear,
    but we believe it was for us
    he hung and suffered there.

3   He died that we might be forgiven,
    he died to make us good,
    that we might go at last to heaven,
    saved by his precious blood.

4   There was no other good enough
    to pay the price of sin;
    he only could unlock the gate
    of heaven, and let us in.

5   O dearly, dearly has he loved,
    and we must love him too,
    and trust in his redeeming blood,
    and try his works to do.

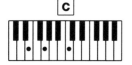  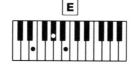 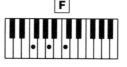 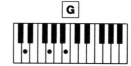

We Plough The Fields

Original Words by M Claudius / English Words by Jane Montgomery Campbell / Music by J A P Schulz

Suggested Registration: Flute
Rhythm: Soft Rock
Tempo: ♩ = 112

We plough the fields and scat - ter the good seed on the land, but it is fed and wa - tered by God's al - migh - ty hand: he sends the snow in win - ter, the warmth to swell the grain, the bree - zes and the sun - shine, and soft, re - fresh - ing rain. *All good gifts a - round us are sent from heaven a - bove; then thank the Lord, O thank the Lord, for all_____ his love.*

1 We plough the fields and scatter
the good seed on the land,
but it is fed and watered
by God's almighty hand:
he sends the snow in winter,
the warmth to swell the grain,
the breezes and the sunshine,
and soft, refreshing rain.

*All good gifts around us
are sent from heaven above;
then thank the Lord, O thank the Lord,
for all his love.*

2 He only is the maker
of all things near and far;
he paints the wayside flower,
he lights the evening star;
the winds and waves obey him,
by him the birds are fed;
much more to us, his children,
he gives our daily bread.

All good gifts . . .

3 We thank thee then, O Father,
for all things bright and good,
the seed-time and the harvest,
our life, our health, our food.
Accept the gifts we offer
for all thy love imparts,
and, what thou most desirest,
our humble, thankful hearts.

All good gifts . . .

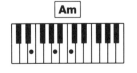
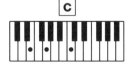

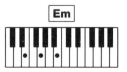
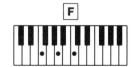
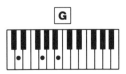

We Sing The Glorious Conquest

Words by John Ellerton / Music from *Württemberg Gesangbuch*

Suggested Registration: French Horn
Rhythm: March
Tempo: ♩ = 108

We sing the__ glor-ious con - quest be - fore__ Dam-as-cus'

gate, when Saul, the__ Church-'s spoil - er, came breath-ing threats and

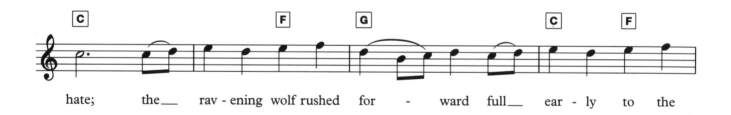

hate; the__ rav-ening wolf rushed for - ward full__ ear-ly to the

prey; but lo, the__ Shep-herd met__ him, and bound him fast to - day.

1   We sing the glorious conquest
before Damascus' gate,
when Saul, the Church's spoiler,
came breathing threats and hate;
the ravening wolf rushed forward
full early to the prey;
but lo, the Shepherd met him,
and bound him fast today.

2   O glory most excelling
that smote across his path!
O light that pierced and blinded
the zealot in his wrath!
O voice that spake within him
the calm reproving word!
O love that sought and held him
the bondman of his Lord!

3   O Wisdom, ordering all things
in order strong and sweet,
what nobler spoil was ever
cast at the victor's feet?
what wiser master-builder
e'er wrought at thine employ
than he, till now so furious
thy building to destroy?

4   Lord, teach thy Church the lesson,
still in her darkest hour
of weakness and of danger
to trust thy hidden power:
thy grace by ways mysterious
the wrath of man can bind,
and in thy boldest foeman
thy chosen saint can find.

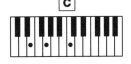
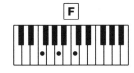
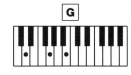

When I Survey The Wondrous Cross

Words by Isaac Watts / Music adapted by E Miller

Suggested Registration: Pipe Organ
Rhythm: Waltz
Tempo: ♩ = 92

When I_____ sur - vey the won - drous

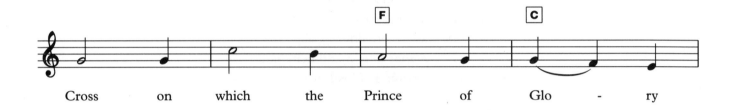

Cross on which the Prince of Glo - ry

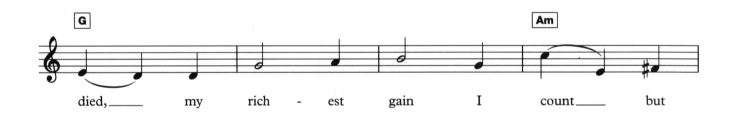

died,_____ my rich - est gain I count____ but

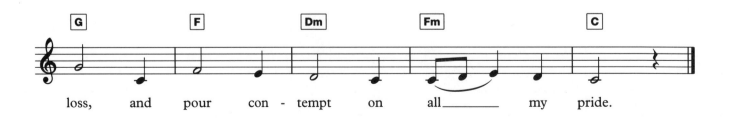

loss, and pour con - tempt on all_____ my pride.

1 When I survey the wondrous Cross
on which the Prince of Glory died,
my richest gain I count but loss,
and pour contempt on all my pride.

2 Forbid it, Lord, that I should boast
save in the Cross of Christ my God;
all the vain things that charm me most,
I sacrifice them to his blood.

3 See from his head, his hands, his feet,
sorrow and love flow mingling down;
did e'er such love and sorrow meet,
or thorns compose so rich a crown?

4 Were the whole realm of nature mine,
that were an offering far too small;
love so amazing, so divine,
demands my soul, my life, my all.

Am

C
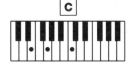

Dm
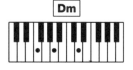

F
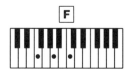

Fm
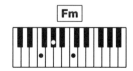

G
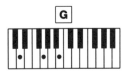

Printed and bound in Great Britain

The Easy Keyboard Library

also available in this series

Country Songs
including:
Don't It Make My Brown Eye's Blue,
Just When I Needed You Most,
The Rose and Stand By Your Man

Classic Hits Volume 1
including:
All Woman, From A Distance,
I'd Do Anything For Love
(But I Won't Do That) and Show Me Heaven

Classic Hits Volume 2
including:
Don't Go Breaking My Heart,
Heal The World,
My Baby Just Cares For Me and
What A Wonderful World

Showtunes
including:
Anything Goes, Forty-Second Street,
I Remember It Well and
Lullaby Of Broadway

Number One Hits
including:
Congratulations, Moon River,
Stand By Me and Without You

Film Classics
including:
I Will Always Love You, Chariots
Of Fire, Aces High and Mona Lisa

Love Songs Volume 1
including:
Careless Whisper,
The First Time Ever I Saw Your Face,
Saving All My Love For You
and True Love

Love Songs Volume 2
including:
I'll Be There, Love Me Tender,
Where Do I Begin? (Love Story) and
You've Lost That Lovin' Feelin'

Christmas Songs
including:
Another Rock & Roll Christmas,
Frosty The Snowman, Jingle Bells and
Mistletoe And Wine

Soul Classics
including:
Fever, My Girl, (Sittin' On) The Dock
Of The Bay and When A Man Loves
A Woman

TV Themes
including:
Birds Of A Feather, Coronation Street, Last
Of The Summer Wine and Match Of The Day

Big Band Hits
including:
Come Fly With Me, In The Mood,
It's Only A Paper Moon and Secret Love

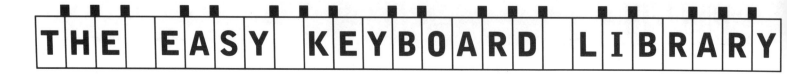

THE EASY KEYBOARD LIBRARY